THIS BOOK BELONGS TO

....

Thank you for being our Valued Customer. We would be grateful If you shared this happy experience on amazon. This helps us to continue providing great products, and helps potential buyers to make confident decisions

www.dreamycoloringbook.com

Dreamy
COLORING BOOK

Have a question? Let us know,
support@dreamycoloringbook.com

COLOR TEST PAGE

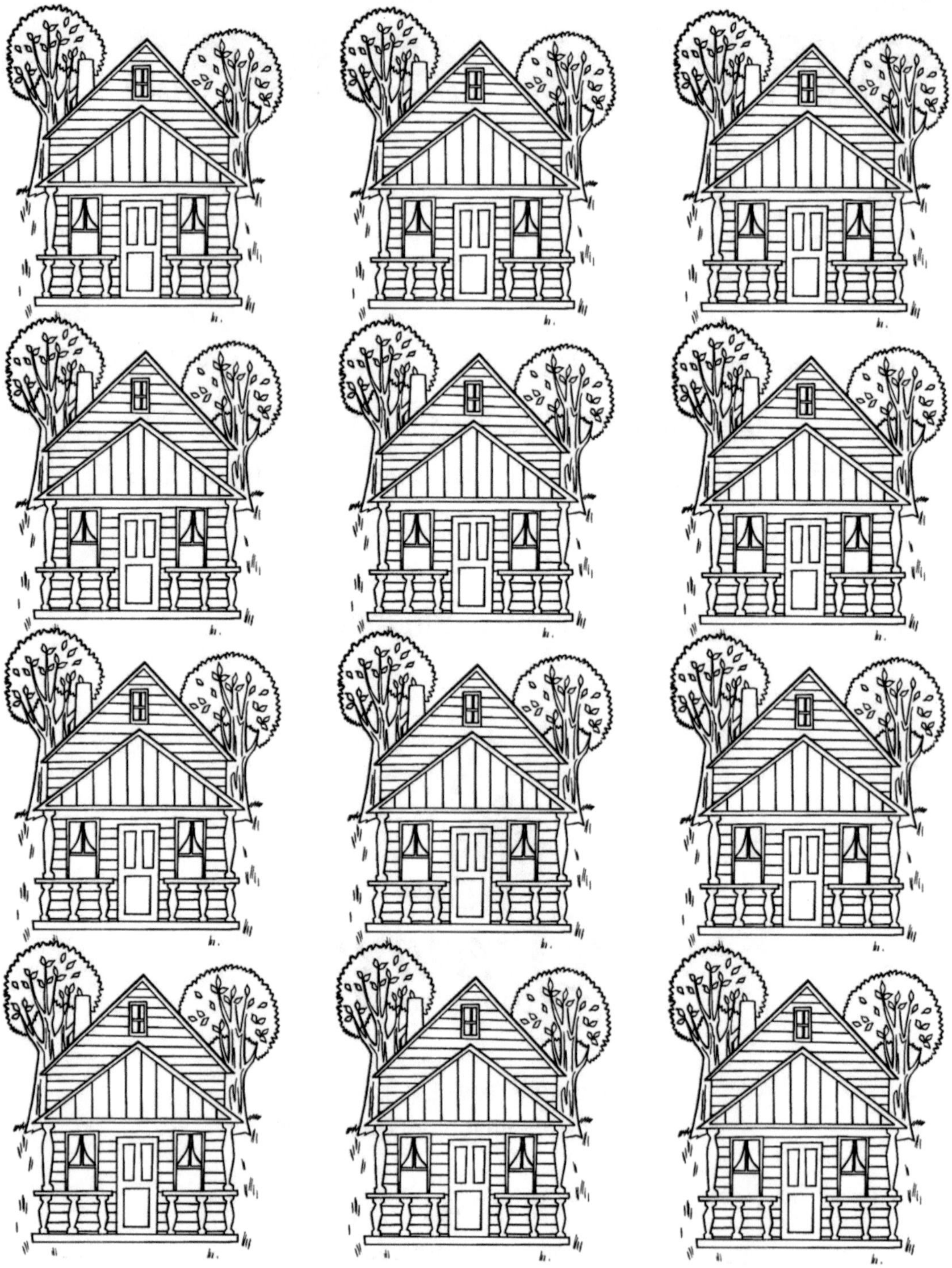

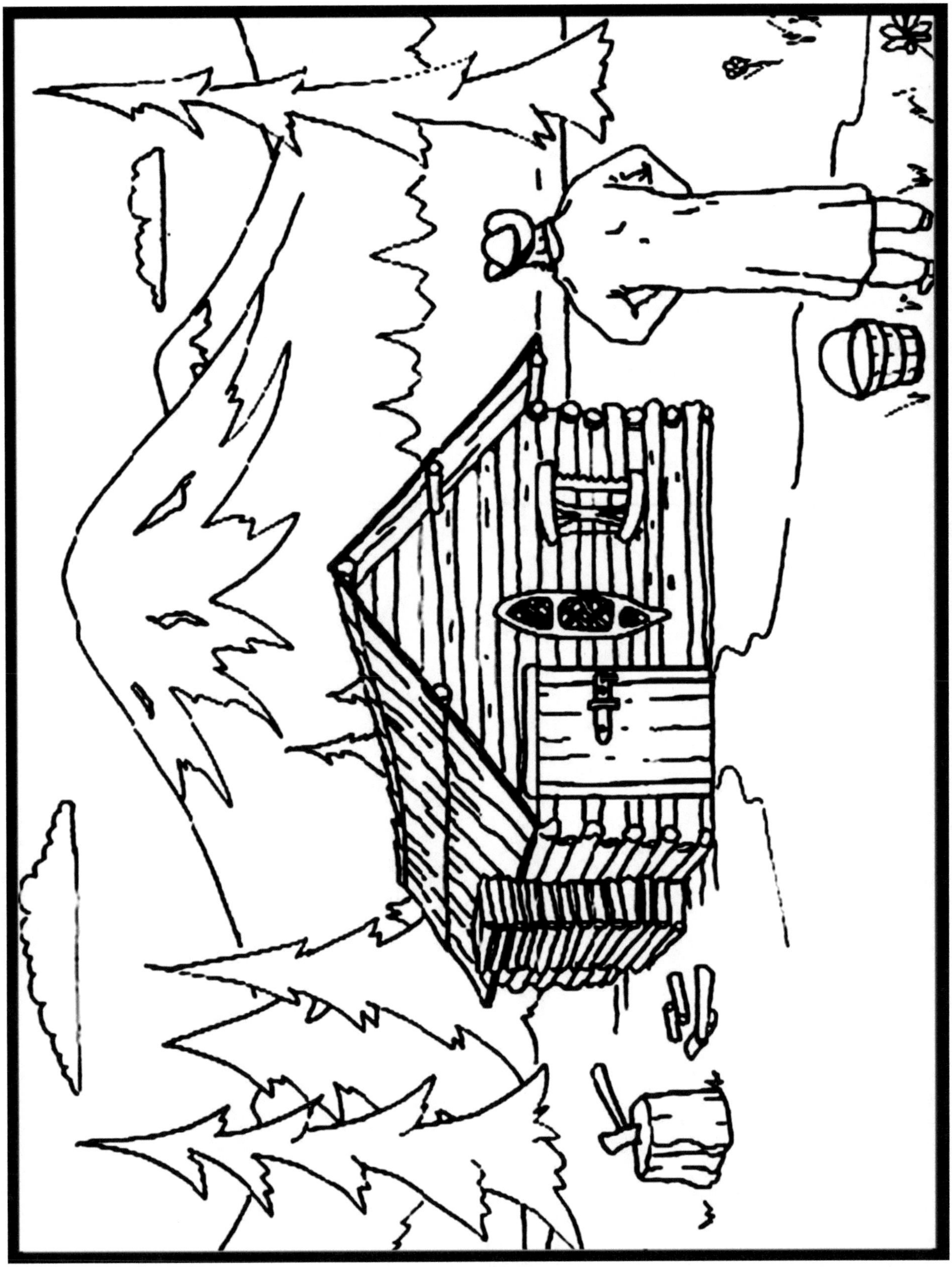

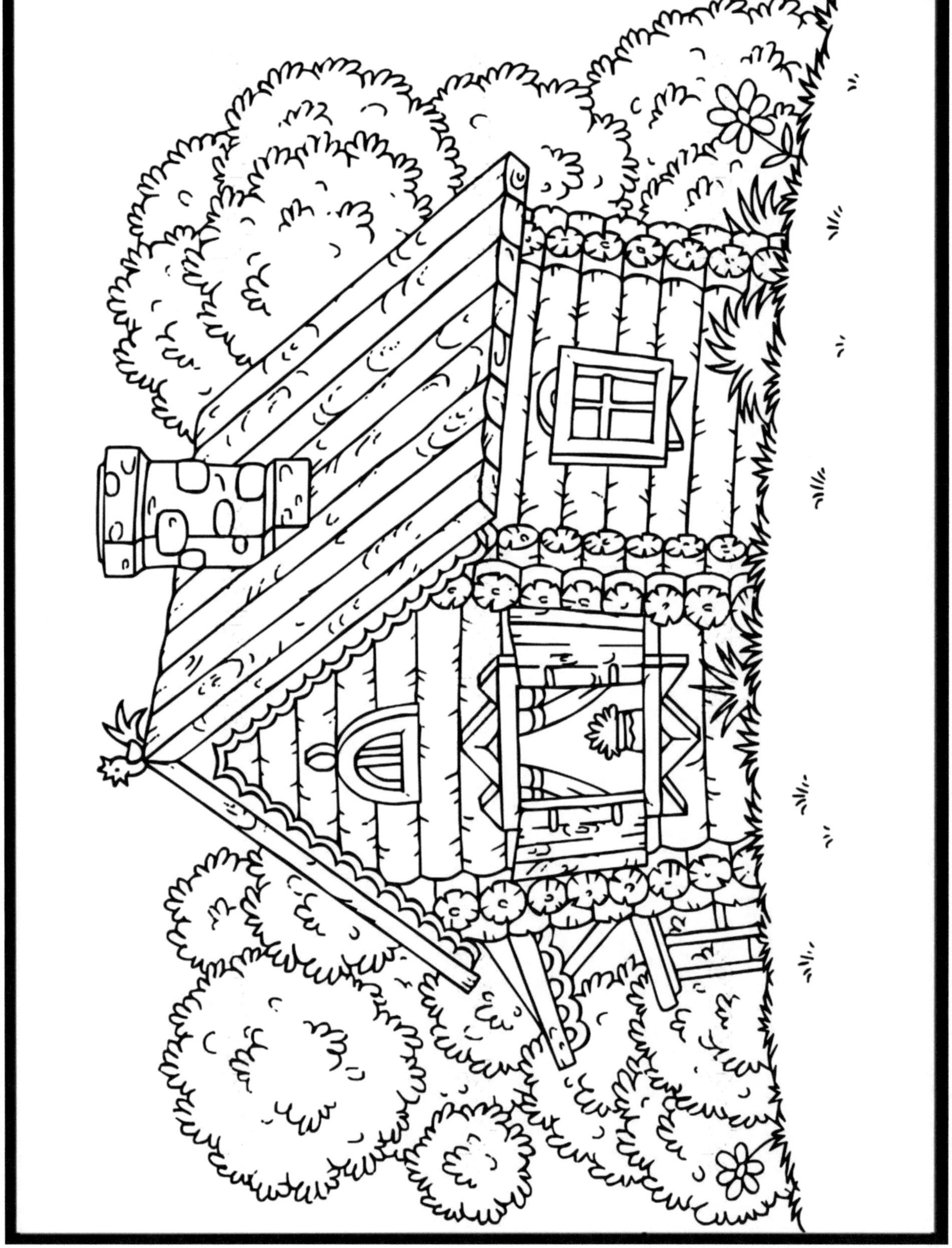

* GLASS
* SNOW

Made in the USA
Thornton, CO
06/10/23 02:16:17

0775d81a-18e7-42d3-b211-e796844d392fR02